Ukutya Kwasekhaya

Tastes from Nelson Mandela's Kitchen

REAL AFRICAN PUBLISHERS

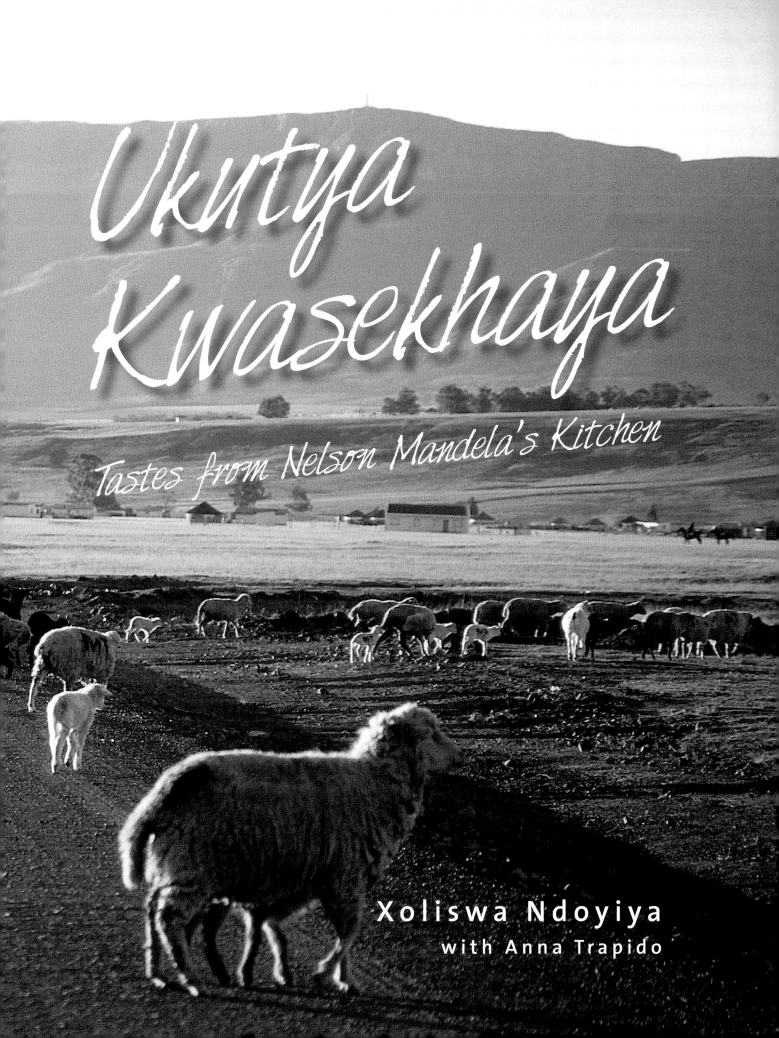

Ukutya Kwasekhaya

Tastes from Nelson Mandela's Kitchen

Xoliswa Ndoyiya

with Anna Trapido

REAL AFRICAN PUBLISHERS

Published by Real African Publishers Pty Ltd
PO Box 3317
Houghton 2041
Johannesburg
South Africa

Tel: +27 11 833 2294
Fax: +27 11 833 2296

First Published in 2011

© Xoliswa Ndoyiya

ISBN 978-1-9869968-1-8

NMF Project Manager:	Ruth Rensburg
RAP Publishing Manager:	Angela McClelland
Writer:	Anna Trapido
Editor:	Sue de Groot
Food stylist:	Hilary Biller
Photography:	Debbie Yazbek
Design:	Adam Rumball
Chef's Assistant:	Nancy Kinyua

NELSON MANDELA CENTRE OF MEMORY
at the Nelson Mandela Foundation
Living the legacy

Thanks to the Nelson Mandela Centre of Memory at the Nelson Mandela Foundation for facilitating the publication of this book.

All recipes herein were prepared and photographed at the HTA School of Culinary Art, Randburg.

Photograph of Qunu, Eastern Cape: Peter McKenzie

Contents

Meat

Breads and desserts

Drinks

For Mkhululi, Sinethemba, Mngophiso
and Lubambo in recognition of how much
they have given up for my working life.
I hope that this book will in some way
show you where I was and what I was
doing all the times I wasn't at home
being your mother.

NELSON MANDELA

Xoli,

Thank you for feeding us

so well all these years.

Mandela

Nelson Mandela Foundation
Chairperson: Prof G J Gerwel, Chief Executive: Mr Achmat Dangor
Founder's Office
Manager Founder's Office: Zelda la Grange
Email: zeldalag@nelsonmandela.org
Tel: 011 728 1000
Fax: 011 728 7878

Acknowledgements

For a long time it was my dream to write a cookbook but I never thought that it would actually happen. There are so many people that I want to thank for helping to turn my dream into a reality. I cook the way I do because of who I am, and I am the way I am because of all those who have loved me.

I want to thank the Mandela and Machel families who have, in so many different ways, been so supportive of this project. I have also received kindness and support from the staff of the Nelson Mandela Foundation, Real African Publishers, Hilary Biller and Debbie Yazbek. Similarly, the help of Nancy Kinyua at the HTA School of Culinary Art was invaluable. I am grateful to Anna Trapido who heard me when I said I wanted to write a book and pushed me to make my dream a reality. I am humbled by the goodness of Sarah Mabulela, who gave up her time so that I could work on my book.

Thank you to Thoko and Jomo Mavuso, who have given me so much warmth that having them was like having a sister and brother in Johannesburg. I am also lucky to have had such a good working relationship with Mr Mandela's bodyguards and medics, many of whom I have known since Shell House days. And to the wonderful ladies who ran Madiba's various offices during all the time I've worked for him: you have always been invaluable in helping me plan meals according to his busy schedule, and I thank you for this.

The faith of my in-laws, the Xongo family, helped give me the confidence to produce this book. The fact that they believed in me enough to give me such a wonderful husband and that they have continued to love and support me even after his tragic death is such a source of strength in my life. My own family, the Ndoyiyas, have encouraged me during times of doubt, when I worried that this book might never happen, and they have taken such good care of my children, which allowed me to work away from home.

Finally, there are many special people without whom I would not be writing this today.

The first is my mother who, when I first went to look for work in Johannesburg as a very young woman, said to me, "You are going to another country. There is no one there to whom you are related and no one who understands from where you have come. So respect people. Respect their differences and remember that not all days in life will be happy." That advice has stayed with me. Without those words of wisdom I think I would have come home, sad and disappointed, and never reached this point in my life.

The second is my sister, Phindiwe, who has been a second mother to my children – looking after them when I could not. Her support, love and friendship have been invaluable to me as a sister and as a mother.

The third is my brother, Stotto, who I still miss so much, but my thanks and gratitude go also to the members of his rugby team, the Shining Stars. When he passed away they said to me, "You mustn't think that your brother is gone – as long as we are here, he is still here." They have been my brothers and whenever I was able to, I have cooked for them like their sister.

The fourth is of course, Madiba, who has always treated me with such kindness and respect. I am so thankful that I have had the opportunity to contribute to his life. I was born three days after Madiba went to jail and, without his long walk, my life and the lives of all South Africans would have been so much worse. I feel privileged to have fed him as President and private citizen.

And fifthly, if it were not for my dear friend, Gloria Nocanda, I would not have met Mr Mandela or been in his life, and I want to thank her more than words can say.

Finally, I want to thank my late husband, Oscar Xongo, who in life was so tolerant and understanding of my frequent work-related absences and even in death is the inspiration for all my best work. He believed in me as a wife and as a mother. He encouraged me in my profession to be the best I can be. He brought such wonderful joy and kindness into my life and that of my children. He was everything to me and he always will be.

Thank you also to friends and family from home, and to all the mothers and fathers of my church, who have always given me their blessings to carry away with me.

I am so pleased and grateful to have had so many special people in my life. I hope you will all feel my love in these words.

Xoliswa Ndoyiya

Foreword

Ever since I started working with President Mandela, Xoliswa Ndoyiya has been there somewhere in the background, caring for him, looking after him, cooking for him. It started with that formidable pair, Xoliswa and Gloria Nocanda. They came with Madiba from the ANC into government; I found them there when I arrived a few days after the inauguration. It was a new world for me and these two strong women from my home province provided the assurance that nobody would take undue liberties in the household. Many are the tales that can be told of how they put some important people in their place.

Xoli – as she is fondly known – is a very gentle person and her devotion to Madiba is legendary. What I personally found so touching over the years is the feeling she always gave me that she assumed the two of us shared that devotion. She would speak to me as a sister speaking about a joint father. Her cries for help when she thought he was in some or other way being offended will remain in my memory as much as the meals she cooked and served over the years.

Many are the luminaries that receive awards and accolades, and as many that benefit from their association with Madiba. Few could, however, have served him with greater loyalty, devotion and consistency than Xoliswa Ndoyiya. They also serve who stand and wait, the saying goes. Stand and wait is not what Xoli did. Cook and wait, more likely. And what wonderful meals she has cooked over the years.

It has been a simple pleasure working with you, Xoli; and a privilege to have you as a partner in service of our Tata. May you enjoy many more years of cooking, sometimes just for yourself and your own enjoyment. You deserve it.

Professor Jakes Gerwel

My Life in Food

I may be known best as Nelson Mandela's personal chef, but I began life as a little girl who liked to make ginger beer and *magwinya* for her family in the Ezibeleni township of Queenstown in the Eastern Cape. Ezibeleni means "place of peace and happiness" in isiXhosa and that is how it felt to me, my sister, Phindiwe and my brother, Stotto.

When I was young I understood that my mother was stirring love into every pot of hot *ulusu* and, even if I didn't always like it, I knew that my paternal grandmother, MaSitatu, was feeding me her hopes and dreams along with her *umkhuphu*.

Those who eat are also affected emotionally by the food. Tata Mandela has told me that every time I make *umphokoqo*, he remembers his mother cooking this dish for him with love. When my third son, Mnqophiso, eats his father's favourite barbequed meat, he thinks of how he would have enjoyed preparing this dish with his late father.

We do not like to speak about personal things in my culture. I always keep painful memories close and quiet, but to understand my food you must know something of my life.

I was born in the Eastern Cape and the first thing I remember eating is mother's *inconco*. This dish is still so much more to me than fermented maize and water. It is love on a spoon. As a child, from the kitchen to my bedroom its strong smell would hit the back of my nose: you can taste it even before it is in your mouth. Even now, if I have had a difficult day, it is *inconco* that I cook to restore calm. I know that I am strong with a bowl of *inconco* in front of me.

In isiXhosa we call home food *ukutya kwasekhaya*, but as I grew older I became curious about the food of other cultures. My maternal grandmother, Uyawathe, was a domestic worker in the kitchen of the Devrin family and I would rush from school to their home knowing that she would

have saved me a small piece of her staff lunch. It wasn't because I was hungry, but for a little girl used to traditional African foods, the buttery mashed potato, spicy *bobotie* and especially the bread-and-butter pudding with raisins seemed so exotic. Sometimes I would chat to my grandmother while she made the Devrins' supper, but mostly I watched and learned by her side. There are recipes from that kitchen that I still use to this day. Every time I grate carrot and pineapple into a salad I remember myself as that little girl. All I knew then was that I liked to cook and that I liked to look after people. Although much has changed in my life, those things have stayed the same.

As is the custom for Xhosa women, my mother insisted that I eat *isidudu* for ten days after the birth of my first son, Mkhululi. I am convinced that in each mouthful was the wisdom and strength of all the Ndoyiya women who came before me. Mkhululi was a source of great joy to us all, especially his uncle Stotto, who, being the only male in our household, was happy to have someone with whom to share his role as man of the house. Mkhululi means "you released me" in isiXhosa, and when his uncle named him he meant that the burden of male responsibility could now be shared between them.

Tragically that burden was not shared but passed on, because my brother was murdered and my little boy became the man of our house long before his time. In Mkhululi I see so much of Stotto's strength, wisdom and kindness. I also see his enthusiasms and talents. My brother was a devoted member of the Queenstown Shining Stars rugby team and I remember how, as a little girl, I would make huge pots of *umngqusho* for him and his friends to eat after a match. That was my way of showing support. Whether they were celebrating a win or facing the disappointment of defeat, that bean and maize stew always went down well. Stotto's team-mates were pallbearers at his funeral and asked us not to bury him in his team blazer. The team manager said, "We are waiting for another of the Ndoyiya boys to wear that jacket." When he does, I hope his sister, Lubambo, is waiting with pots of *umngqusho* to celebrate the moment.

My first kitchen job was with the Rothston family in Johannesburg. It was not a grand start. Mostly I was the potato peeler and dishwasher, but there has to be a beginning. I am eternally grateful to close family friend, Miriam Ngcbicibi, who not only recommended me to the Rothstons but also helped me through my anxious first few months in the big city and taught me how to cook kosher food. After I left the Rothstons I was employed at a Jewish old people's home, because I could make chopped liver and potato latkes. If you like the Jewish recipes in this book, you should congratulate Paulette Rothston and Miriam Ngcbicibi, who taught me well.

Johannesburg has been good to me, but love and joy are seldom experienced without a mirror of pain. In 1992 I was three months pregnant when my second son's father, Eric Sizani, who was working as an ANC security official, disappeared. Though his body was never found we were told that he was murdered by Inkatha warlords. I called my baby Sinethemba, which means "we have hope", and it was a long time before I gave up hope of seeing this sweet, good man alive. We shared so little of my pregnancy before his disappearance, but I can never eat a plum without thinking of the happiness that the idea of our baby brought him. I remember that I craved sour plums in those first few weeks of pregnancy. It was the wrong time of year for plums, but Eric searched every grocery store in the city and came home triumphant with boxes and boxes of them. Sinethemba has that same sweetness and concern for the wellbeing of others. He has grown into a boy who fills so many hopes and dreams. His father would have been so proud of him, as are we all.

Even in moments of extreme sadness, opportunities arise. As I mourned Eric's death, my friend, Gloria Nocanda, called me to say that she was working for Nelson Mandela and wanted me to join her in the kitchen. This was a time before South Africa's first democratic election and Madiba had only recently been released from prison. Gloria arranged for me to be picked up and taken to meet with the ANC security officials. There was a strict background check and interview, which I must have passed because I was taken straight in to see Madiba, who said, "I believe that you are a great cook, but can you cook our food?" I replied that I could cook *ukutya kwasekhaya*. And that was that.

When I was first employed I didn't know how it would be, but I understood that the job was to cook for Nelson Mandela himself. One day, quite soon after I arrived, he called us from the kitchen and asked Gloria and me how we would feel about also taking care of his grandchildren.

He said that he knew the ANC had employed us just to look after him, but that imprisonment had deprived him of the experience of watching his own children grow up and he would like to have his grandchildren close by. Of course we said we were happy to give him this chance and so Mandla, Ndaba, Mbuso, Rochelle and Andile came to stay. Madiba was so busy with elections and then the presidency, but he loved coming back to that noisy house filled with children. He still does. We all do.

I catered everything from family reunions to late-night political strategy sessions, and so began the relationship with Madiba and his family that continues to this day. Any household with such a range of ages at the dinner table is a challenge for the cook. Madiba is happiest with traditional food – if you don't give it to him for a few days he will ask, "What's wrong? Why are you not feeding me well?" The children grew up under different circumstances, so there had to be birthday cakes and burgers as well as *umxhaxha* and *amasi*.

Through it all my life has gone on. When I met Oscar Xongo on a bus travelling between Queenstown and Johannesburg, love was the last thing on my mind, but from this meeting came much joy and two children. We were married in 2001 in Butterworth. The icing roses on my wedding cake matched my lemon-yellow suit. We had left it very late to get a cake and when we saw the perfect one, the lady in the cake shop didn't want to sell it to us – it was so pretty that she wanted to keep it in the window to attract customers. But she saw how much we wanted it and eventually let us buy it.

As is our custom, the Xongo family gave me a new first name to mark my new marital status. I became Noxhanti, which means "pillar", and I hope that I have done justice to the strength of that name.

Oscar loved my cooking – if I was at work and other people offered to cook for him, he would say "No, let's wait for Noxhanti." One day in 2006 he was driving home to us when he was killed in a car crash. We miss him so much and the gap he left still hurts every day, but we are all better people for having known him. The roses on our wedding cake are long gone, but there is a yellow and white wreath at the point on the road where he died, and the joy we experienced together in picking out that cake will stay with me forever.

I have loved working for Tata and the Mandela family, but there are, of course, sacrifices that come with such a task. I am in Johannesburg while my family remains in Queenstown. I miss my mother, Nozilandu; my sister, Phindiwe; my children, Mkhululi, Sinethemba, Mnqophiso and Lubambo; and my nieces, Sanelisiwe, Onele and Sanele. Every day I miss them. There are children here who call me mama, which helps with the pain of separation – I am also bonded with the Mandela children. I am always with them and I am recognised as a mother by them, and that's how I feel about them. But sometimes my own children have suffered as a result of my absence. There have been times when Lubambo has been ill and I couldn't be there. My boys are rugby players and there are many tries that I have not been there to see and to celebrate with them. My mother and sister have done a wonderful job of raising my children and, for all of them, I hope this book will show them where I was and why it was worthwhile.

I have cooked everywhere, from kosher kitchens to palaces, and I have always wished to bring peace and happiness into everything I do. Some people don't see cooking as important, but I truly believe that we who stir pots and roast meats have a big responsibility. Chefs bring whatever love, longing, sadness and joy they feel to the stove and it goes into their food. This is a power that should not be taken lightly, either by those who cook or those who eat.

There are certain dishes the Mandela family members love so much that they have me making them all the time, but this book has also been a way for me to explore other dishes. Because of the emotional significance of the recipes, I want to show them exactly as I have always made them, not make them fancy. I am not ashamed to say that I use stock cubes, Aromat seasoning and margarine, because that is what tastes good and feels right to me. If I take them out and hide the fact that I use them I am removing my secret tricks from you. This book is not about secrets, it is about sharing. These are recipes from a real South African kitchen; they celebrate simple tastes in a complicated world.

My food memories are very personal. It is hard for me to put them into words, and even harder to explain in a recipe how much that dish means to me and to others, but I hope that this book will give you a taste of my times.

From left to right: Mkhululi Ndoyiya, Sanelisiwe Ndoyiya, Onele Ndoyiya, Mnqophiso Ndoyiya-Xongo, Nozilandu (Violet) Ndoyiya, Xoliswa Ndoyiya, Phindiwe (Portia) Ndoyiya, Lubambo Ndoyiya-Xongo, Sanele Ndoyiya, Sinethemba Ndoyiya

Whenever I go home to visit my children, they get to choose what I cook for the first four days. The first night's choice is Mkhululi's, and he will always pick something hot: he loves curry and spicy things. On the second night Sinethemba chooses, and I know it will be his favourite sweet chicken. On the third night we will usually have lasagne, because my third son Mnqophiso is mad about pasta – he would be happy to eat it every day. And on the fourth night my daughter, Lubambo decides. She loves anything that mummy cooks, but especially roast lamb.

Soup

"Comfort is just a mouthful away"

Pea soup

Zindzi Mandela, Nelson Mandela's daughter, says: *My father has vested a lot of trust in Sis' Xoli and he gets anxious if she's not there. It's not difficult to see why – her food is always so comforting. Her cooking makes a home out of a house. With every bowl of soup you just know that however tough life might be, comfort is just a mouthful away. And you have no idea how much we appreciate it.*

Serves 4 – 6

500g frozen peas
400g (2 medium) potatoes, peeled and chopped
1 chicken stock cube
500ml (2 cups) water
1 medium onion (about 100g), finely grated
125ml (½ cup) fresh cream
45ml (3 tbsp) olive oil
salt and white pepper, to taste

Put the peas, potatoes, stock cube and water in a pot. Bring to the boil, reduce heat and cook until the potatoes are soft, about 20 minutes. Add a little extra liquid if necessary.
Remove from the heat and blend to a purée.
Add the onion and cook for a few minutes.
Add the cream and cook over a low heat. Add additional liquid if too thick. Stir in the oil and slowly bring to the boil. If its still too thick, stir in a little boiling water.
Season and serve.

Isophu (sugar bean and white maize soup)

Isophu is another one of those tastes that we all grew up with. In the early 1990s, before he was President, Tata used to come back from work at Shell House (the former ANC headquarters), sometimes with Tata (Walter) Sisulu or sometimes Uncle Raymond Mhlaba and they would smell that I was cooking isophu or umfino (spinach and maize meal porridge) and they would say, "Aah, ukutya kwasekhaya, home food" and be very happy with it.

Serves 8 – 10

700g dried sugar beans
3 chicken stock cubes (or to taste)
2,5 litres water
300g white maize (corn), cleaned and removed from the cob
1 medium onion (about 100g), finely chopped
30ml (2 tbsp) butter
salt and white pepper, to taste

Place the beans, stock cubes and water in a pot, bring to the boil, then reduce heat and simmer until the beans are soft, about 2 hours. During this time a nice brown stock will form. Add extra water when necessary to prevent the beans from sticking to the bottom of the pot.
Once the beans are soft, add the maize kernels, onion and butter and cook until you have a thick, wholesome soup, about a further 30 minutes. Season and serve hot.

Butternut soup

Luvuyo Mandela, Nelson Mandela's great-grandson, says: *I grew up in Durban, so when I came to Jo'burg to visit my great-grandfather, Mum' Xoli was like a mother to me. Whenever I came she would make me do the things that little boys sometimes forget, like having a bath. Sometimes I was naughty and disregarded her advice, but she never stopped loving me. I remember when Michael Jackson came to the house. I was about nine years old and I was going through a silly craze where I thought it was cool not to wear socks under my shoes. Mum' Xoli made me put on socks, but as soon as I was around the corner I took them off. Every time I see the photo of me with Michael Jackson, there I am with shoes but no socks, and I think of how she tried to make me look as if I came from a good home.*

Serves 6 – 8

1kg butternut squash, peeled, rinsed, seeded and roughly chopped
2 litres water
1 medium onion (about 100g), finely grated
3 chicken stock cubes (or to taste)
500ml (2 cups) fresh cream
salt and white pepper, to taste

Put the butternut into a large pot with the water and bring to the boil. Reduce the heat and cook the butternut until the water has reduced by a third and the butternut is soft enough to mash, about 20 minutes.
Transfer the butternut and liquid to a food processor and blend to form a smooth purée. Add the onion and stock cubes and blend again. Return the mixture to the pot and cook gently over a medium heat until the onion is cooked through, about 2 minutes.
Add the cream and warm gently. Add a little milk or extra stock dissolved in water if the soup is too thick. Season and serve.

Vegetable soup

Madiba loves this soup – especially with a bit of pepper. Actually, he says he likes "a bit of pepper" but in terms of most people's tastes it's a lot of white pepper that he wants. Our mouths all react differently to pepper and his likes to feel it strongly. If you want to taste it the way Madiba does, give the pepper pot a very generous shake and wait for the back of your throat to glow!

Serves 8 – 10

1 medium (about 100g) onion, chopped
5 large carrots (about 400g), peeled and chopped
4 medium potatoes (about 800g), peeled and chopped
300g green beans, chopped
3 celery sticks with leaves, chopped
500g butternut squash, peeled, seeded and chopped
200g baby marrows, chopped
150g broccoli florets
3 litres water (or to cover)
2 vegetable stock cubes
salt and white pepper, to taste
fresh flat-leaf parsley, to garnish

Combine the vegetables, water and stock cubes in a large pot. Bring to the boil, reduce heat and cook until the potatoes are soft, about 20 minutes.
Blend the soup until completely smooth.
Season and serve garnished with the parsley.

Brown and green lentil soup

Ndileka Mandela, Nelson Mandela's granddaughter, says: *Everything Xoliswa cooks is just exceptional. She has given us recipes and we all try to make her dishes at home but it's not the same. She has a secret way of putting that extra pinch of love into the sauce.*

Serves 4 – 6

200g (1 cup) green lentils, soaked in water
for 1 hour before cooking
200g (1 cup) brown lentils, soaked in water
for 1 hour before cooking
75ml olive oil
1 medium onion (about 100g), finely chopped
2 garlic cloves, finely chopped
1 medium potato (about 200g), peeled and
grated
2 large carrots (about 150g), peeled and grated
1 litre water
2 chicken stock cubes
salt and freshly ground black pepper, to taste

Drain and rinse the lentils and cook them in enough water to cover until soft, about 15 minutes. Drain and return to the pot.
Heat the oil in a large pot and fry the onion and garlic over a low heat until the onion is soft and golden, about 5 minutes.
Add the onion mixture to the lentils together with the potato, carrots, water and stock cubes and cook until the vegetables are soft, about 15 minutes.
If too thick, feel free to thin out with extra water or stock for a smoother, soupier texture
Season and serve.

Spinach soup

Mbuso Mandela, Nelson Mandela's grandson, says: *Wow. What can you say about Mum' Xoli's food? Every soup, every stew – they all come with love. That's what you can say. Her food always leaves the mouth craving. You can taste the love and you just want more!*

Serves 6 – 8

60ml (¼ cup) olive oil
1 medium onion (about 100g), finely chopped
2 garlic cloves, finely chopped
3 medium potatoes (about 600g), peeled and finely chopped
4 large carrots (about 300g), grated
300g spinach, finely chopped
2 chicken stock cubes
2 litres water
125ml (½ cup) fresh cream, to serve (optional)

Heat the oil in a pot and sauté the onion until soft and golden, about 5 minutes.
Add the garlic, potatoes and carrots and cook over a medium heat until soft, about 10 minutes.
Add the spinach and cook for 2 minutes.
Add the stock cubes and water and bring to the boil. Reduce heat and cook for a further 30 minutes.
Blend until smooth, season and serve hot with a swirl of cream, if desired.

Chicken soup

I first made this soup for Mbuso (Madiba's grandson) when he had to have his tonsils out. He was a very little boy and Madiba was so worried about him. They are very close, those two, because the child was raised in this house with his grandfather from a baby. On the morning of the operation Madiba had to be in Cape Town for Parliament, but as soon as he came home to Johannesburg he drove straight to the hospital.

Serves 4 – 6

45ml (3 tbsp) olive oil
2 medium onions (about 200g), finely chopped
1 garlic clove, finely chopped
5ml (1 tsp) paprika
300g skinless chicken fillets, cut into strips 1cm thick and 5cm long
3 medium tomatoes (about 250g), grated
1,5 litres water
2 chicken stock cubes
60ml (¼ cup) fresh parsley, finely chopped

Heat the oil in a pot and fry the onion, garlic and paprika until the onion is soft and golden, about 5 minutes.
Add the chicken and cook through over a medium heat for about 5 minutes.
Add the tomatoes, water, stock and parsley and cook until you have a thick, wholesome soup, about 20 minutes.
Season and serve hot. (For those with sore tonsils, first blend smooth.)

Peanut butter and spinach soup

I made this for Madiba's grandson, Mandla and his brothers when they were little because I felt they should eat peanut butter, which is good for you, but whenever it came out of the cupboard they would say they didn't like it. So I hid it in the soup, which they loved. Even when Mandla was a teenager he ate the soup, and they still love it.

Serves 4 – 6

60ml (¼ cup) olive oil
1 medium onion (about 100g), grated
2 medium potatoes (about 400g), peeled and grated
4 large carrots (about 300g) carrots, grated
600g spinach, finely chopped
1,25 litres (5 cups) water
2 chicken stock cubes
30ml (2 tbsp) smooth peanut butter
salt and white pepper, to taste

Heat the oil in a pot and sauté the onion until soft and golden, about 5 minutes.
Add the potatoes, carrots and spinach and mix to combine. Add the water and stock cubes and bring to the boil. Reduce heat and cook until the potatoes are soft, about 15 minutes.
Add the peanut butter, mix well and cover the pot with a lid. Simmer on a low heat for a further 10 minutes.
Season and serve.

Prawn soup

Dr Ike Kwame Amuah, Nelson Mandela's son-in-law, says: *There is so much one can say about Xoli and her cooking. She is blessed with excellent culinary skills and is a natural talent.*

Serves 4 – 6

250g prawns, shelled and cleaned
1 medium onion (about 100g), finely chopped
2 garlic cloves, finely chopped
1 medium potato (about 200g), peeled and grated
2 large carrots (about 150g), grated
2 medium tomatoes (about 150g), grated
2 chicken stock cubes
500ml (2 cups) water
60ml (¼ cup) fresh cream
60ml (¼ cup) olive oil
salt and white pepper, to taste
cooked prawns, tails intact, to serve (optional)

Place the prawns in a pot together with the onion, garlic, potato, carrots, tomatoes, stock cubes and water. Bring to the boil, then reduce the heat and simmer for 20 minutes.

Blend until smooth, adding a little water if the soup is too thick. Stir in the cream and 45ml (3 tbsp) of the oil.

Heat the remaining oil in a pan and fry the remaining prawns until cooked through, about 5 minutes.

Season the soup and serve hot, topped with the extra prawns if desired.

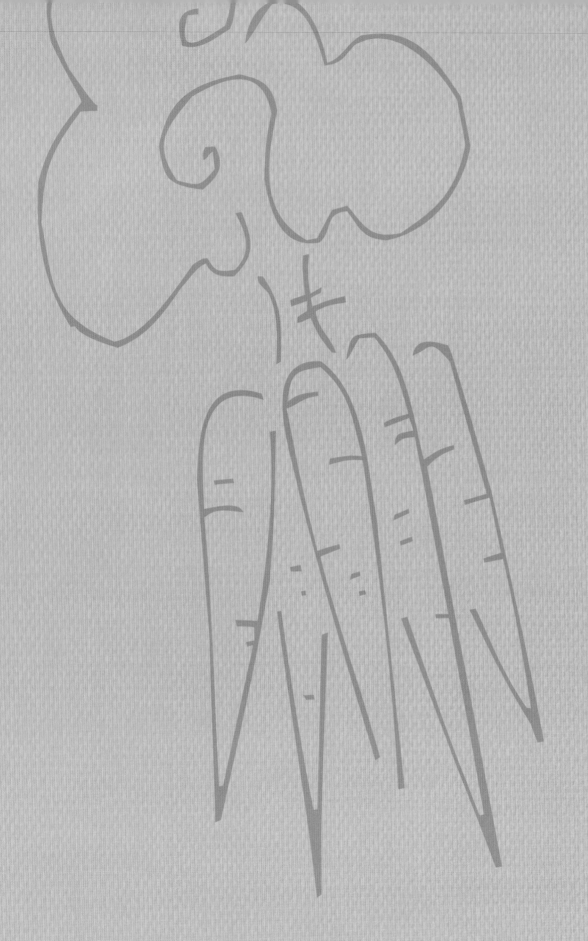

Vegetables

"Andilohashe"
("I'm not a horse")

Umqa wekhaphetshu
(stiff maize meal porridge with curried cabbage)

Tata (Walter) Sisulu always used to want meat. Meat, meat, meat – if you tried to give him salads he would say "andilohashe" which means, "I'm not a horse" in isiXhosa. But this rule didn't apply when it came to the vegetables of his childhood – he always cleared his plate when there was umqa wekhaphetshu and other traditional Xhosa vegetable dishes.

Serves 6 – 8

1 cabbage (about 1,7kg), finely shredded
1,5 litres water
2 chicken stock cubes
1 small onion (about 50g), finely chopped
4 spring onions, chopped
30ml (2 tbsp) mild curry powder
240g (2 cups) white maize meal
60ml (¼ cup) butter
salt and white pepper, to taste

Place the cabbage, water and stock cubes in a pot, cover with a lid and bring to the boil, then reduce the heat and cook until the cabbage is soft, about 10 minutes.
Add the onion and spring onions and cook for a further 2 minutes.
Add the curry powder and maize meal and stir constantly over a low heat until all the liquid is absorbed, about 5 minutes. The stirring is essential to prevent lumps.
Add the butter and stir through, then cover the pot with a lid and cook over a low heat until the maize meal is cooked through, about 30 minutes. Season and serve hot with grilled chicken or lamb chops.

Umngqusho (samp and beans)

In many Xhosa households, Wednesday is umngqusho day. It's the way we all grew up. Like Fridays in the Eastern Cape are always dumplings with meat day. Even if it's not a Wednesday, Tata gets sad if days go by and I haven't cooked umngqusho. He will call me to come and ask "Where's umngqusho?" In this recipe I have used butter, but in rural communities people often use what Jewish families call schmaltz and we call amafutha enkuku (chicken fat left over from cooking) to add a richness at the end of the dish.

Serves 6 – 8

500g samp (crushed maize), well rinsed
800g dried sugar beans, well rinsed
water, to cover
2 beef stock cubes
salt and white pepper, to taste
45ml (3 tbsp) butter or amafutha enkuku

Place the samp and beans in a pot, cover with water and bring to the boil, then reduce the heat and cook until soft, at least 2 hours. Do not stir or it will become excessively starchy, but keep checking to see that the mixture is not sticking to the bottom of the pot and add water if necessary. After about 1 hour add the stock cubes. When the mixture is soft and cooked through, strain off the remaining water.
Season and stir in the butter.
Serve with boiled meat such as umleqwa.
(see recipe on page 108).

Umfino (maize meal porridge with spinach)

Albert Ndlovu, Mandela family handyman and gardener, says: *She cooks everything so nice but her pap, yoh, it's good. You know, we black people, our most favourite dish when we grew up was pap. Rice was scarce but pap... we are experts in pap! And she knows very well how to prepare it. Some people, they prepare it and it has those nasty little pimples in it, but not Sis' Xoli. Her pap is nice and soft. And when she adds vegetables. Yoh. Lekker!*

Serves 6 – 8

30ml (2 tbsp) vegetable oil
1 small onion (about 50g), finely chopped
4 spring onions, finely chopped
1kg spinach, chopped
500ml (2 cups) water
120g (1 cup) white maize meal
salt and white pepper, to taste

Heat the oil in a deep pot and fry the onion and spring onions until soft, about 5 minutes.
Add the spinach and half a cup of the water. Cook over a high heat until the spinach has wilted, about 2 minutes.
Add the remaining water and bring to the boil, then pour in the maize meal and stir vigorously to prevent lumps.
Once all the water is incorporated, cover the pot and cook over a low heat until the maize is done, about 10 minutes.
Season and serve.

Umphokogo

(crumbly maize meal porridge and sour milk)

When American comedian, Bill Cosby came to visit, he heard the word, umphokoqo, which of course he struggled to say. He tried and failed and said, "You people click and click as if you are eating peanut butter".

Serves 6 – 8

500ml (2 cups) water
5ml (1 tsp) salt
360g (3 cups) maize meal
amasi (sour milk, see recipe on page 158), to serve

Bring the water and salt to the boil in a pot. Add the maize meal, cover with a lid and bring back to the boil.
Once it is boiling, stir the porridge with a fork until the water is absorbed. This will create a nice rough texture.
Cover the pot again, reduce the heat and cook until the porridge is soft, about 25 minutes.
Serve with amasi on the side so that each person can stir in their own amount according to taste.

Umxhaxha (corn and pumpkin)

Nkosi Zwelivelile Mandela, Nelson Mandela's grandson and Chief of the Mvezo Traditional Council, says: *It is in dishes like this that Sis' Xoli reminds us where we are from and who we are as a family. In food she links us to the Thembu nation.*

Serves 4 – 6

3 white mielies (corn on the cob), shucked and cleaned
500ml (2 cups) water
1kg pumpkin, peeled, seeded and diced
15ml (1 tbsp) sugar (if the pumpkin is sweet you can do without the sugar)

Remove the corn kernels from the cobs.
Bring the water to the boil in a pot and cook the corn for 10 minutes.
Add the pumpkin and cook until the vegetables are soft and all the water has evaporated. Mash to form a nice chunky mixture.
Add sugar according to taste and serve.

Umkhuphu (beans with maize meal)

Nelson Mandela's granddaughter, Tukwini Mandela says: *She's been our friend, our mother, our confidant. We've all sat in my grandfather's kitchen and I have learned all sorts of things there. Not just about cooking and food but about life in general. When I have visited my grandfather, the kitchen has always been my first port of call. If I was unsure or upset or frightened – or if something really good had happened – that was where I went first. The thing is, you always know you will get the truth from Sis' Xoli, whether you like it or not! I am particularly grateful for the way that she has helped us younger members of the family to know and understand my grandfather better. Her grace and insights have improved our relationship with him.*

Serves 6 – 8

500g dried sugar beans, well rinsed, or other dried beans (this is the dried weight; they are heavier when soaked)
120g (1 cup) white maize meal
water, to cover
salt, to taste

Place the beans in a pot, cover with water and bring to the boil, then reduce the heat and cook until soft, at least 2 hours. Add more liquid when necessary.
Add the maize meal, making sure there is enough liquid left (about 1 cup) to cook the maize meal. If necessary add water.
Cover the pot and cook over a low heat until the water is absorbed and the porridge is soft, about 20 minutes.
Stir, season and serve.

Tshakalaka (spicy relish)

This always reminds me of my first-born son, Mkhululi, who cooks very well. He can make a sauce from nothing. He often sits and watches me and we talk about cooking. But he loves, loves, loves hot things. The other kids say, "Please don't let bhuti (brother) cook for us because it will be hot, hot, hot!"

Serves 8 – 10

125ml (½ cup) cooking oil
2 medium onions (about 200g), finely chopped
1 x 410g tin baked beans in tomato sauce
3 medium tomatoes (about 240g), peeled and finely chopped
1 medium green pepper (about 80g), seeded and chopped
1 medium red pepper (about 80g), seeded and chopped
4 large carrots (about 280g), grated
10ml (2 tsp) peri-peri powder or
5ml (1 tsp) cayenne pepper
1 vegetable stock cube

Heat the oil in a large pan and fry the onions until soft and golden, about 5 minutes.
Add all the other ingredients and cook over a low heat for about 30 minutes, stirring occasionally, until a thick relish has formed. Reduce the amount of peri-peri powder if you prefer it milder.
Serve hot with maize meal porridge and/or grilled meat.

French beans

Nkosi Zwelivelile Mandela, Nelson Mandela's grandson, says: *Sis' Xoli has given up so much to look after us. Sometimes I feel that we Mandela children have benefited at the expense of her own kids. They are far away in the Eastern Cape while she is with us. But we all – my grandfather, myself, all of us – are so thankful for her role in our lives. We would be lost without her.*

Serves 6 – 8

250g rindless back bacon, fat removed and cut into large pieces
30ml (2 tbsp) butter
1 medium onion (about 100g), finely chopped
1kg green beans, sliced at a slant
2,5ml (½ tsp) fresh rosemary, finely chopped
250g button mushrooms, thickly sliced
salt and white pepper, to taste.
50g mature Cheddar cheese, grated, to serve

Fry the bacon until crisp and set aside.
Melt the butter in a pan and fry the onion until tender, about 2 minutes. Add the beans, bacon and rosemary.
Cover the pan with a lid and cook over a low heat until the beans are tender, about 5 minutes.
Add the mushrooms and cook for about 3 minutes.
Season and serve hot with the cheese sprinkled over.

Potato latkes

Before I worked for Madiba I was the cook at a Jewish old-age home. I still make recipes I learned there. Good food is good food, and this recipe is as popular in the Mandela house as it was with the Jewish old ladies.

Serves 8 – 10

40g (⅓ cup) cake flour
7,5ml (1,5 tsp) baking powder
3 medium potatoes (about 600g), peeled and grated, excess liquid squeezed out
2 medium onions (about 200g), peeled and grated
5ml (1 tsp) Aromat seasoning
2 large eggs, lightly beaten
250ml (1 cup) cooking oil, for frying

Sieve the flour and baking powder into a bowl. Add the potatoes, onions and Aromat and mix until well combined. Mix in the beaten egg a little at a time until you have a thick batter that drops off a spoon. You may not need all the egg. Heat the oil in a pan and drop tablespoons of the batter into the pan. Fry in batches until the latkes are golden brown on both sides. Drain on paper towel.
Serve immediately while still hot and crisp.

Pumpkin fritters

Luvuyo Mandela, Nelson Mandela's great-grandson, says: *In the hustle and bustle of modern life, Mum' Xoli has a way of cooking that is traditional and comforting, but requires real patience. She doesn't make quick fixes. They aren't dishes you will find in a restaurant, which is why when friends invite me out to dinner there is often a sense of disappointment that I can't just stay in and eat what Mum' Xoli has cooked.*

Serves 8 – 10

2,5kg pumpkin, peeled, seeded and diced
40g (⅓ cup) cake flour
7,5ml (1,5 tsp) baking powder
sugar, to taste (optional)
1 large egg, beaten
cooking oil, for frying

Cook the pumpkin in boiling salted water until soft, about 15 minutes. Drain, mash and allow to cool completely.
Add the sieved flour and baking powder to the cooled pumpkin and mix well. Add a little sugar if you want the fritters to be sweeter.
Gradually beat in the egg until you have a thick batter of dropping consistency.
Heat the oil in a pan and drop in tablespoons of the batter. Fry on both sides until golden and cooked through.
Serve immediately.

Filled gem squash

Ndaba Mandela, Nelson Mandela's grandson, says: *Mum' Xoli is a person with lots of compassion. She is so kind and open and you can taste it in everything she cooks. It's true of everything she makes – you really taste the love.*

Serves 8

4 medium gem squash, cut in half, seeds removed
100g bacon, chopped
1 medium green pepper (about 80g), seeded and finely chopped
1 medium red pepper (about 80g), seeded and finely chopped
90g mature Cheddar cheese, grated
5ml (1 tsp) paprika

Cook the gem squash in salted boiling water until tender, about 20 minutes.
Preheat the oven to 180°C.
Fry the bacon in a pan until crisp. Add the peppers and fry for a further 2 minutes.
Fill each squash cavity with the bacon mixture, top with the cheese and sprinkle with a little paprika.
Place the filled squash on a baking tray, cover loosely with foil and bake for 10 minutes.
Serve hot.

Aubergine salad

Nelson Mandela's granddaughter, Zoleka Mandela says: *I think of uSis' Xoli's cooking and I'm instantly reminded of all the most amazing and heartfelt conversations we've had as a family gathered around the dinner table at my grandfather's home in Houghton. I think about all the times we've had second servings of her cooking and debated on which of her dishes are the most scrumptious and irresistible. I will always have this beautiful image of her in the kitchen literally pouring love into her meals. She's always smiling and owns one of the biggest hearts I know and gives the warmest hugs. Her food is much like her personality; it's an emotional source that connects us to each other at the most happy and even most tragic of times.*

Serves 6 – 8

60ml (¼ cup) olive oil
4 large aubergines, cut into rounds 3cm thick
4 medium tomatoes (about 350g), sliced
into rounds
200g mozzarella ball, sliced into rounds
5ml (1 tsp) dried oregano
5ml (1 tsp) dried thyme
5ml (1 tsp) lemon juice
salt and white pepper, to taste

Heat about 30ml (2 tbsp) of the oil in a large pan and fry the aubergines on both sides until soft and golden.
Arrange the aubergines on a platter alternating with the tomatoes and mozzarella
Mix together the remaining oil with the oregano, thyme and lemon juice. Season and pour over the salad to serve.

Fried butternut

My friend, Thoko has been a pillar of strength to me over many years. She is a good colleague and a friend, but if I talk to her it's like she is my own sister. She's straightforward – if you are wrong you are wrong; if you are right you are right. I have learnt so much from her. That's how she is.

Xoliswa's friend, Thoko Mavuso says: *I love those sweet butternut cubes. If Xoli is cooking them I sit in the kitchen and taste and taste while she is cooking. I can't help it, because they are just like little mouthfuls of heaven on a plate.*

Serves 6 – 8

1kg butternut, peeled, seeded and cubed
45ml (3 tbsp) sunflower oil
30ml (2 tbsp) butter
45ml (3 tbsp) golden syrup
5ml (1 tsp) ground cinnamon

Cook the butternut in boiling water until it is cooked through but still firm. Drain.
Heat the oil and butter in a pan and fry the butternut until golden, about 5 minutes.
Add the syrup and cinnamon and toss well.
Serve hot.

Lemon Brussels sprouts

Nandi Mandela, Nelson Mandela's granddaughter, says: Xoliswa sprinkles even the simplest dishes with love and affection. Even things I normally think I don't like, I love when she prepares them.

Serves 6 – 8

450g Brussels sprouts, cleaned and trimmed
30ml (2 tbsp) margarine or butter
10ml (2 tsp) lemon zest
salt and white pepper, to taste
lemon rind, finely grated, to serve (optional)

Cook the sprouts in salted boiling water until tender, about 8 minutes.
Drain off the water and add the remaining ingredients. Cook for 5 minutes, stirring occasionally.
Serve hot, garnished with lemon rind if desired.

Creamed spinach

Co-author, Anna Trapido says: *Like everything Xoli cooks, her creamed spinach has a retro-chic motherly generosity. There's no poncy nonsense. You feel a million mothers at a million dinner tables in every spoon.*

Serves 8 – 10

125ml (½ cup) water
400g spinach, stems removed and chopped
10ml (2 tsp) butter
60ml (¼ cup) olive oil
1 medium onion (about 100g), grated
30ml (2 tbsp) cake flour
250ml (1 cup) fresh cream
60g mature Cheddar cheese, grated
salt and white pepper, to taste

Boil the water in a pot and cook the spinach with the lid on for 5 minutes. Drain off any remaining water and set aside.

In a separate pot, heat the butter and oil and fry the onion until soft and golden, about 5 minutes. Add the flour and stir until well combined. Cook for 2 minutes, then add the cream and cook for a few minutes, stirring until slightly thickened. Add the cheese and cooked spinach and mix well. Season and serve.

Curried mango
rice salad

We served this at my wedding to Oscar Xongo. I love its bright colours and the sweet memories it brings back for me. It is such a sunny, friendly recipe, full of joy.

Serves 6 – 8

440g (2 cups) basmati rice, rinsed
2,5ml (½ tsp) salt
2 ripe mangoes, peeled and cubed
375ml (1,5 cups) mayonnaise
30ml (2 tbsp) mild curry powder
15ml (1 tbsp) fresh parsley, finely chopped
salt and white pepper, to taste

Put the rice and salt in a pot of cold water, bring to the boil, reduce the heat, cover with a lid and simmer until cooked through, about 10 minutes. Drain, rinse and set aside to cool.
Once the rice is cool, mix in the mangoes.
Mix together the mayonnaise, curry powder and parsley and fold this into the rice mixture. Season and refrigerate until ready to serve.
If you like, garnish with a sprig of fresh flat-leaf parsley and a slice of mango.

Savoury rice

Nelson Mandela's friend and comrade, Amina Cachalia, who is a frequent lunch guest, recently wrote a letter to Xoliswa saying: *Thank you, Xoli, for always being so pleasant and graceful and prompt and for not allowing me to clear up after a splendid meal.*

Serves 6 – 8

440g (2 cups) basmati rice, rinsed
2,5ml (½ tsp) salt
60ml (¼ cup) olive oil
1 medium onion (about 100g), finely chopped
3 large carrots (about 220g), peeled and
finely grated
1 medium red pepper (about 80g), seeded and
finely chopped
1 medium green pepper (about 80g), seeded and
finely chopped
15ml (1 tbsp) dried oregano
1 chicken stock cube
250ml (1 cup) water

Put the rice in a pot with the salt and cover with water. Bring to the boil and cook for 5 minutes, then rinse and drain. Set aside.
Heat the oil in a large pan and fry the onion over a medium heat until golden, about 5 minutes.
Add the carrots, peppers and oregano and fry until the peppers are soft, about 5 minutes.
Add the stock cube and water and bring back to the boil, then reduce the heat.
Add the rice, cover with a lid and simmer over a low heat until the rice is cooked through, about 10 minutes.
Serve garnished with a sprig of fresh flat-leaf parsley, if desired.

Carrot and pineapple salad

This recipe comes from my grandmother. She worked for the Devrin family for many years and this was one of her recipes that she made for them. We eat this with chicken or boerewors (sausage) and mash.

Serves 8 – 10

4 large carrots (about 300g), finely grated
1 medium pineapple, peeled and finely grated
500ml (2 cups) fresh orange juice
5ml (1 tsp) lemon juice
orange slices, to serve

Mix together the carrots, pineapple, orange and lemon juice and refrigerate for about 1 hour so that the flavours can infuse.
Serve garnished with the orange slices.

Creamy potatoes

Oprah Winfrey loves these potatoes. Last time she came she said to me, "I came straight from the airport. I didn't stop anywhere because I needed Xoli's potatoes." She comes into the kitchen and when she sees what I am doing she claps her hands and says, "Aaahhhh, Xoli's potatoes!"

Serves 6 – 8

4 medium potatoes (about 800g), peeled and cut into rounds about 1cm thick
125ml (½ cup) olive oil
2 medium onions (about 200g), peeled and cut into thin rings
250ml (1 cup) fresh cream
10ml (2 tsp) Aromat seasoning

Preheat the oven to 180°C.
Cook the potatoes in salted boiling water until tender but firm, about 10 minutes. Drain and set aside to cool.
Heat the oil in a pan and fry the onions until soft and golden, about 5 minutes. Remove the onions from the pan with a slotted spoon and set aside.
Fry the potatoes in the same pan until golden on both sides.
Arrange alternate layers of potato and onion in one large ovenproof dish or in individual ramekins.
Mix the cream and the Aromat together and pour over the potatoes and onions.
Bake until the potatoes are cooked through and the top is golden, about 30 minutes.
Serve hot.

Fish and seafood

"We are the
fish girls in
the family"

Whole baked fish

Nandi Mandela, Nelson Mandela's granddaughter, says: *I love Xoliswa's pink fish. My sister and I are the fish girls in the family. We love it. I have tried making it at home but it's not the same – hers has some secret. I don't think she is holding out on us, it's just that really good cooks have an instinct, and she definitely has it.*

Serves 6 – 8

MARINADE
60ml (¼ cup) freshly squeezed lemon juice
15ml (1 tbsp) crushed garlic
30ml (2 tbsp) mixed spice for fish
60ml (¼ cup) olive oil
45ml (3 tbsp) peri-peri powder (or dried chilli flakes)

1 medium (about 1,5kg) firm-fleshed sea fish
1 medium onion (about 100g), sliced into rings
2 medium tomatoes (about 150g), sliced into thin rings

Mix all the marinade ingredients together in a large container. Make 3 shallow cuts on each side of the fish and immerse in the marinade.
Leave to marinate for 15 minutes.
Preheat the oven to 180°C.
Remove the fish from the marinade and place in an oven dish. Place the onion and tomato slices on top of the fish. Cover with foil and bake for 45 minutes.
Remove the foil and cook for a further 5 minutes. (If you prefer your fish crispy, remove the foil earlier.)
Serve with tomato and onion salad and side dishes of your choice.

Late-start starter

*In my work you sometimes need a delaying tactic. The office will call and say,
"Sorry, sorry, but we are sending five people for lunch." And it's 12:15 and they are
set to arrive at 12:30. So then I make this starter, because while they are eating it
I have time to quickly make the main course.*

Serves 6

6 small hake steaks
15ml (1 tbsp) lemon juice
15ml (1 tbsp) mixed spice for fish
125ml (½ cup) sunflower oil
30ml (2 tbsp) cake flour
2 large eggs, beaten
24 small prawns, peeled and cleaned
(pre-cooked and frozen will work)
30ml (2 tbsp) mayonnaise
15ml (1 tbsp) fresh parsley, finely chopped
salt and white pepper, to taste
3 avocados, peeled, halved and sliced to
form a fan
1 carrot, peeled and cut into strips
6 curly lettuce leaves
1 tomato, thinly sliced
1 cucumber, thinly sliced
6 black olives
1 lemon, thinly sliced

Rub the hake steaks with the lemon juice and
fish spice.
Heat the oil in a large pan.
Roll the hake steaks in the flour to coat well, then
dip in the egg and fry in the hot oil until cooked
through and golden brown on both sides.
Set aside.
Cook the prawns in boiling water for 5 minutes
(if pre-cooked, just parboil until heated through),
then toss with the mayonnaise and parsley
and season.
To serve, place a hake steak and 4 prawns on
each plate along with half a fanned avocado.
Garnish with a few carrot strips, a lettuce leaf, a
slice of tomato, a slice of cucumber, an olive and
a twist of lemon.

Prawn curry

Limpho Hani, a frequent visitor to the Mandela house, says: *I have been fortunate enough to have been invited to several private lunches with Tata and Aunt Graça. My memory is of amazing food and a wonderful relaxed atmosphere where we laughed. The meals are always delectable, prepared with love and passion. I loved everything, but my particular favourite was Xoliswa's prawns.*

Serves 6 – 8

60ml (¼ cup) olive oil
2 medium onions, finely chopped
5 medium tomatoes (about 400g), peeled, seeded and grated
15ml (1 tbsp) crushed garlic
15ml (1 tbsp) hot curry powder
2,5ml (½ tsp) paprika
2,5ml (½ tsp) peri-peri powder
(or dried chilli flakes)
2kg prawns, peeled and cleaned
125ml (½ cup) water
salt and white pepper, to taste
60ml (¼ cup) fresh coriander, chopped, plus extra to serve
basmati rice, cooked, to serve

Heat the oil in a large pan and fry the onions until soft and golden, about 5 minutes.
Add the tomatoes, garlic, curry powder, paprika and peri-peri powder and cook over a low heat until a thick sauce forms, about 5 minutes.
Add the prawns and water and bring to the boil, then reduce the heat, cover with a lid and simmer over a low heat for about 20 minutes.
Season and stir in half the coriander.
Serve with basmati rice, garnished with the extra coriander.

Seafood spaghetti stir-fry

Ndileka Mandela, Nelson Mandela's granddaughter, says: *This is the most divine dish. It's healthy and it's not heavy. Divine, divine, divine. I like to cook and I have copied it at home, and people are always complimentary, but mine is never quite as nice as Sis' Xoli's.*

Serves 8 – 10

200g spaghetti, broken into 5cm pieces
125ml (½ cup) sunflower oil
500g hake, cut into 2cm strips
45ml (3 tbsp) cake flour
1 large egg, beaten
60ml (¼ cup) olive oil.
1 medium onion (about 100g), finely sliced
1 medium red pepper (about 80g), seeded and sliced
1 medium yellow pepper (about 80g), seeded and sliced
50g (1 cup) cabbage, finely shredded
3 large carrots (about 220g), peeled and cut into thin strips
5 baby marrows (about 160g), cut into thin strips
100g spinach, finely shredded
60ml (¼ cup) soy sauce
5ml (1 tsp) Aromat seasoning
salt and white pepper, to taste

Cook the spaghetti in salted boiling water until tender. Drain and set aside.
Heat the sunflower oil in a frying pan.
Dip the fish into the flour to coat well, then into the egg, then fry in the hot oil until golden on both sides.
In a separate pan, heat the olive oil and fry the onion until soft and golden, about 5 minutes. Add the peppers, cabbage, carrots and baby marrows and fry until cooked through, about 5 minutes. Add the spinach and fry for a minute, then stir in the soy sauce, Aromat, spaghetti and fish. Adjust seasoning to taste.
Mix well and serve hot.

Paella

Grandson, Kweku Mandela Amuah says: *I love Ma' Xoli's food because it is made with the love, caring and joy she shows me every time I see her ... and ultimately it tastes good.*

Serves 8 – 10

600g (3 cups) long-grain rice
5ml (1 tsp) turmeric
125ml (½ cup) sunflower oil
400g hake, cut into 2cm squares
15ml (1 tbsp) mixed spice for fish
60g (½ cup) cake flour
1 large egg
80ml (⅓ cup) olive oil
1 medium onion (about 100g), finely sliced
250g marinara mix (mixed seafood: calamari, mussels, etc)
16 prawns, peeled and cleaned
1 medium red pepper (about 80g), seeded and cut into thin strips
1 medium green pepper (about 80g), seeded and cut into thin strips
1 medium yellow pepper (about 80g), seeded and cut into thin strips
150g brown mushrooms, sliced
5ml (1 tsp) fresh thyme, leaves only
salt and white pepper, to taste

Cook the rice with the turmeric in salted boiling water until tender, then drain and set aside.
Heat the sunflower oil in a pan. Rub the fish with the fish spice, then coat with the flour and dip in the egg and fry until crisp and golden on all sides.
In a separate pan, heat the olive oil and fry the onion until soft and golden, about 5 minutes.
Add the marinara mix and prawns and stir-fry until cooked through, about 5 minutes.
Add the peppers and mushrooms and mix well, then stir in the rice and fish.
Sprinkle with thyme, season and serve.

Poultry

"I'm a wife
because of her"

Peri-peri chicken

Housekeeper to the Mandela family, Sarah Mabulela, says: *Sis' Xoliswa, eish. The way she makes this sauce is something lovely. When she makes it I watch what she is doing and then I go home and I try it. And my husband benefits from what I have learned. I am a wife because of her.*

Serves 6 – 8

MARINADE
30ml (2 tbsp) olive oil
100ml lemon juice
45ml (3 tbsp) water
4 garlic cloves, finely chopped
30ml (2 tbsp) mixed spice for chicken
10ml (2 tsp) paprika
30ml (2 tbsp) mild peri-peri sauce (or mild chilli sauce)
5ml (1 tsp) peri-peri powder (or dried chilli flakes)
30ml (2 tbsp) fresh parsley, chopped

3 baby chickens, butterflied

Mix all the ingredients for the marinade and rub this all over the chickens to coat well. Leave to marinate for 15 minutes.
Preheat the oven to 180°C.
Remove the chicken from the marinade and place in an ovenproof dish. Pour half the marinade over the chicken.
Bake until tender and cooked through, about 45 minutes. The sauce will have reduced to a delicious coating.
Place the remaining marinade in a saucepan and boil for at least 5 minutes.
Serve the chicken with the hot marinade poured over it.

Chicken liver spread

I made this when working at the Jewish old-age home and it is one of the recipes that I have carried with me into my cooking for Tata.

Serves 6 – 8

125ml (½ cup) sunflower oil
2 medium onions (about 200g), chopped
500g chicken livers
2 chicken stock cubes, dissolved in 250ml (1 cup) of boiling water
salt and white pepper, to taste
4 large eggs, hard-boiled, to serve
fresh flat-leaf parsley, finely chopped, to serve

Heat half the oil in a frying pan and fry the onions until soft and golden, about 5 minutes. Remove the onions from the pan and set aside. Add the remaining oil to the pan, heat and fry the chicken livers until cooked through and browned.

Mix the livers and onions together. Add the stock and blend until you have a smooth spread. Season and spoon into a serving dish.

Separate the boiled egg white from the yolk and grate them separately. Arrange the grated egg white, yolk and parsley on top of the liver spread. Serve with Melba toast or crackers.

Peri-peri chicken livers

This is a South African peri-peri recipe rather than the Mozambican version, and the whole family loves it. Zelda la Grange, Nelson Mandela's executive assistant, especially loves it – she says she will do anything for me if I make it for her.

Zenani Mandela, Nelson Mandela's daughter, says: *Xoli has been with my father since he came out of prison. She has been there in so many ways, in more than just cooking. She's like a daughter to him, and to all of us she is family. We all call her Mama or Aunty. She mothered my children and my nephews. She is so special – I am always calling the house and saying 'Am I cooking this right?' And we will spend 30 minutes on the phone. Even then her food is somehow different from mine. Her chicken livers are superb. Even when she talks me through how to do it, no one can beat her cooking.*

Serves 6 – 8

60ml (¼ cup) olive oil
1kg chicken livers
3 medium onions (about 300g), finely chopped
6 garlic cloves, finely chopped
3 medium tomatoes (about 240g) tomatoes, roughly grated
125ml (½ cup) tomato sauce (ketchup)
5ml (1 tsp) dried oregano
5ml (1 tsp) peri-peri powder (or dried chilli flakes)
15ml (1 tbsp) peri-peri sauce (or chilli sauce)
15ml (1 tbsp) mixed spice for chicken
salt and white pepper, to taste

Heat 45ml (3 tbsp) of the oil in a pan and fry the livers until brown, about 2 minutes on each side. Set aside.
Heat the remaining oil in a separate pan and fry the onions and garlic until golden and soft, about 5 minutes.
Add the cooked chicken livers to the onion mixture. Add the tomatoes, tomato sauce, oregano, peri-peri powder, peri-peri sauce and spice. Mix well and cook over a low heat until a thick, rich sauce has formed, about 25 minutes. Season and serve with potato bread on the side (see recipe on page 146).

Sweet chicken

Nandi Mandela, Nelson Mandela's granddaughter, says: *If you want to see a Mandela move fast, wait for the sweet chicken to be ready. Xoliswa puts it on the table and we all look at each other. We have to wait for the elders to go first and then we move in. If you aren't quick it's all gone. It's definitely a competition!*

Serves 4 – 6

5ml (1 tsp) paprika
2,5ml (½ tsp) white pepper
10ml (2 tsp) mixed spice for chicken
1 whole chicken (about 1,25kg), cut into 8 pieces
325ml (1,5 cups) sweet fruit chutney
250ml (1 cup) mayonnaise
30ml (2 tbsp) medium curry powder
250ml (1 cup) water

Preheat the oven to 180°C.
Combine the paprika, pepper and chicken spice and rub the chicken pieces all over with this mixture. Place in an ovenproof dish and roast for 15 minutes.
While the chicken is cooking, combine the chutney, mayonnaise, curry powder and water and mix well to form a sauce.
Remove the chicken from the oven and cover it with the sauce.
Lower the oven temperature to 160°C and roast the chicken until golden brown and cooked through, about 30 minutes.
Serve with rice, garnished with a sprig of fresh flat-leaf parsley if desired.

Garlic chicken

Josina Machel, Graça Machel's daughter, says: *I think we Machels have influenced Sis' Xoli and her use of garlic! Our Mozambican taste buds love to marinate in garlic and our palates have influenced her. In the beginning she was quite careful with it, but we pushed her to add more and more to marinades. That garlic chicken is so, so good. She has really learned about us and our palates.*

Serves 4 – 6

MARINADE
10ml (2 tsp) peri-peri sauce (or chilli sauce)
60ml (¼ cup) olive oil
60ml (¼ cup) lemon juice
6 garlic cloves, crushed to a fine paste
60ml (¼ cup) fresh parsley, finely chopped
30ml (2 tbsp) spice mix for chicken

1 whole chicken (about 1,25 kg), cut into 8 pieces

Preheat the oven to 180°C.
Combine all the marinade ingredients and rub all over the chicken to coat well. Cover and set aside to marinate for at least 30 minutes.
Roast the chicken in a casserole dish in the oven until cooked through and crisp, about 1 hour.
Serve with rice and steamed vegetables or side dishes of your choice.

Boiled Umlegwa (farm chicken)

When I make this for Madiba I have to be very sure that there is umhluzi (traditional meat gravy) in a cup next to his plate. If you don't give him the umhluzi he says, "ibingaseli na?" (was the animal not drinking?). What he means is that the meat is too dry.

Serves 6 – 8

1 large farm chicken (about 2kg), cut into 8 pieces
1 medium onion (about 100g), roughly chopped
750ml (3 cups) water
30ml (2 tbsp) cake flour
salt and white pepper, to taste

Place the chicken portions, onion and 500ml (2 cups) of the water in a large pot and bring to the boil, then reduce heat and simmer uncovered over a medium heat until the chicken is cooked through, about 30 minutes.

Whisk the remaining water with the flour to make a paste and add this to the chicken. Continue cooking until a thick gravy forms, about 10 minutes.

Season and serve with umngqusho (see recipe on page 48) or dombolo (see recipe on page 144).

Chicken curry

Nelson Mandela's granddaughter, Swati Dlamini says: *Her food is so good, I've tried to copy her recipes at home but they never turn out the way hers do. There is nothing that she does that I can possibly say is bad – all her food is delicious. When we are going down to the Eastern Cape the thing I look forward to the most is her chicken.*

Serves 4 – 6

15ml (1 tbsp) mixed spice for chicken
5ml (1 tsp) paprika
5ml (1 tsp) peri-peri powder (or dried chilli flakes)
1 chicken (about 1,25kg), jointed, or
8 chicken pieces
60ml (¼ cup) olive oil
1 medium onion (about 100g), finely chopped
5 medium tomatoes (about 400g), grated
30ml (2 tbsp) mild curry powder (or according to taste)
250ml (1 cup) water
handful fresh coriander
salt and white pepper, to taste

Preheat the oven to 180°C.
Mix the chicken spice, paprika and peri-peri powder together and rub this all over the chicken pieces.
Place the chicken in an ovenproof dish and roast until golden, about 20 minutes.
While the chicken is roasting, heat the oil in a large pot and fry the onion until soft and golden, about 5 minutes. Add the tomatoes and curry powder and mix well. Cook over a low heat until you have a thick sauce, about 5 minutes.
Remove the browned chicken pieces from the oven, drain off the fat and add the chicken to the onion mixture, together with the water. Bring to the boil, then reduce heat, cover and cook gently for 15 minutes.
Add the coriander and simmer for a few more minutes.
Season and serve with rice, garnished with extra coriander if desired.

Chicken and mushroom casserole

Grandson, Zondwa Mandela says: *I have had the pleasure of experiencing Sis' Xoli's cooking for nearly two decades of my life, which qualifies me to state that she is a fantastic cook. My fondest memory is when Sis' Xoli made snacks for my cousins and me 'before' lunch. I say this because at home we have strict and defined eating times: breakfast, lunch and dinner. After a long day of sports we went home to my grandfather's house, with a hunger like that of a black hole in space. Sis' Xoli saw this hunger in our eyes and out of nowhere she rustled up delicious food. Only a mother knows her children to this extent, and through the love and compassion of her cooking she has always made me feel like a son.*

Serves 6–8

1 chicken (about 1,25kg), jointed, or
8 chicken pieces
5ml (1 tsp) mixed spice for chicken
5ml (1 tsp) paprika
250ml (1 cup) ready-made cream
of mushroom soup
1 chicken stock cube, dissolved in 250ml (1 cup)
boiling water
250g white button mushrooms, sliced

Preheat the oven to 180°C.
Rub the chicken pieces all over with the chicken spice and paprika and arrange skin-side up in a casserole dish.
Place in the oven and roast until browned, about 15 minutes.
Mix the soup, stock and mushrooms, pour over the chicken and return to the oven until cooked through, about 30 minutes.
Serve hot.

Creamy chicken with Italian herbs

Bambatha Mandela, Nelson Mandela's grandson, says: *The thing about Xoliswa's food is that she just has that special touch – even when you have finished you want to take a finger and mop up every last little bit of sauce left on the plate. Boy, does she have a way with chicken!*

Serves 4 – 6

1 chicken (about 1,25kg), jointed, or 8 chicken pieces, excess fat removed
15ml (1 tbsp) mixed spice for chicken
60ml (¼ cup) olive oil
1 medium onion (about 100g), finely chopped
250ml (1 cup) fresh cream
125ml (½ cup) water
125ml (½ cup) tomato purée
10ml (2 tsp) dried Italian herb mix (thyme, basil, marjoram, oregano)
10ml (2 tsp) dried oregano
salt and white pepper, to taste

Preheat the oven to 180°C.
Place the chicken in a casserole dish and rub the pieces all over with the chicken spice and the oil. Roast until brown, about 15 minutes.
Drain off any excess oil, add the onion and return the casserole dish to the oven until the onion is soft, about 10 minutes.
Mix together the remaining ingredients and pour over the chicken. Return to the oven and roast until the chicken is cooked through and a thick, creamy sauce has formed, about 30 minutes.
Serve hot.

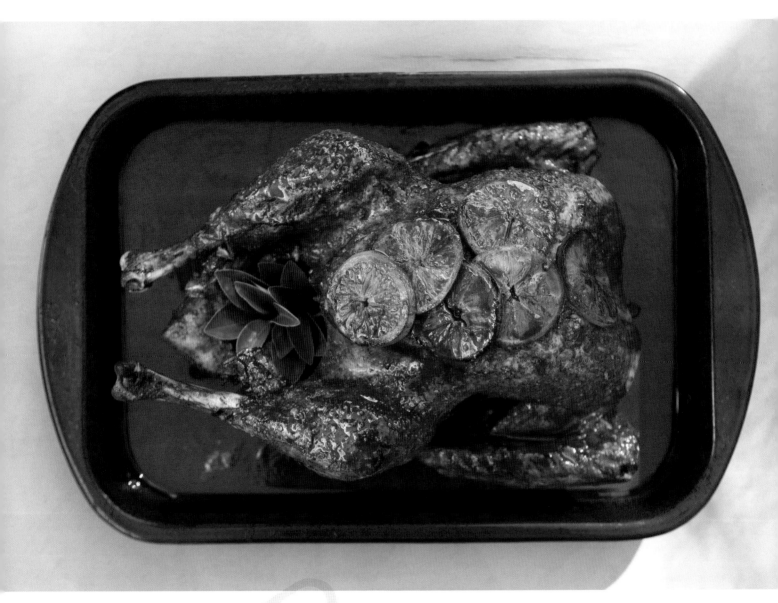

Orange turkey

For me this is the taste of Christmas in Qunu. Everyone relaxes, no one stands on ceremony. They eat and laugh and when they are finished they all bring their own plates into the kitchen.

Serves 8 – 10

MARINADE
750ml (3 cups) fresh orange juice
125ml (½ cup) lemon juice
30ml (2 tbsp) paprika
45ml (3 tbsp) allspice
15ml (1 tbsp) Aromat seasoning
30ml (2 tbsp) mixed spice for chicken

1 turkey (medium)
15ml (1 tbsp) butter, melted
1 orange, thinly sliced

Mix all the marinade ingredients together in a large container. Add the turkey, coat well and leave to marinate for at least 1 hour.
Preheat the oven to 180°C.
Remove the turkey from the marinade, rub all over with the butter and place breast-side down in a roasting dish. Pour over half the marinade, cover with foil and roast for 45 minutes.
Remove the foil and turn the turkey over. Arrange the orange slices on top, pour over the remaining marinade and bake until brown and cooked through, about 1 hour 30 minutes (or depending on weight of the turkey).
Allow to rest before carving and serve with side dishes of your choice.

Meat

"Only Sis' Xoli
can take us to
the ancestors"

Ulusu (tripe)

Everyone in the Mandela household has loved this dish from birth. Maki loves it so much, she always asks me to wrap some up for her to take home.

Mike Maponya, Mr Mandela's senior bodyguard, says: *Sis' Xoli's tripe is a wonderful thing — it has its own unique taste. Every time I taste it I know I am reaching out to ancestors long gone; I know they tasted what I am tasting. Sometimes I go to town and buy it in a restaurant, but it's not the same. Only Sis' Xoli can take us to the ancestors.*

Serves 8 – 10

1kg lamb tripe
750ml (3 cups) water, or to cover
10ml (2 tsp) salt
1 medium onion (about 100g), chopped

Clean the tripe thoroughly and wash well. Cut it into 2cm x 2cm cubes and trim off any excess fat. Put the tripe in a pot with enough water to cover it. Add the salt and onion and bring to the boil, then reduce the heat and cover, leaving a gap for the steam to escape. Simmer until the tripe is very soft, about 2 hours. The liquid will reduce and the onion will caramelise to form a thick gravy.
Serve hot with dumplings, umngqusho or pap.

Umsila wenkomo

(oxtail stew)

Close friend and comrade, Ahmed Kathrada says: *From the first time I had her oxtail, every time I was invited to lunch there I was just wishing it would be oxtail and nothing else.*

Serves 8 – 10

3kg oxtail, excess fat removed
5ml (1 tsp) paprika
15ml (1 tbsp) barbeque spice
5 large carrots (about 350g) carrots, peeled and sliced
250g green beans, sliced
4 medium potatoes (about 800g), peeled and quartered
60g (1 packet) oxtail soup powder
salt and white pepper, to taste

Put the oxtail in a large pot and add just enough water to cover. Bring to the boil, then reduce the heat and cook until the water has evaporated. The meat will start to brown in its own fat. Add the paprika and barbeque spice together with enough water to cover the oxtail. Cover with a lid and cook over a low heat until the oxtail is tender, about 2 hours. Keep checking that there is still enough liquid to cover the meat, adding more water when necessary.
Add the carrots, beans, potatoes and soup powder and cook until the vegetables are soft, about 30 minutes. Season and serve.

Lasagne

Thoko Mavuso, Xoliswa's friend and colleague, says: *I have known Xoliswa for the last 20 years and for all those years I have watched her preparing food for Mr Mandela's family, heads of state, celebrities, prominent people, ordinary people ... and I love everything she cooks. My absolute favourite dish is her lasagne. The flavour just knocks out my tongue – it has something more than its Italian origin. Up to this day I can't enjoy anyone else's lasagne.*

Serves 8 – 10

15ml (1 tbsp) olive oil
2 medium onions (about 200g), finely chopped
4 medium tomatoes (about 320g), peeled, seeded and grated
125ml (½ cup) tomato sauce (ketchup)
60ml (¼ cup) tomato purée
1kg lean beef mince
2 large carrots (about 150g), peeled and finely chopped
2 medium red peppers (about 160g), seeded and finely chopped
2 medium green peppers (about 160g), seeded and finely chopped
1 x 225g tin baked beans
30ml (2 tbsp) dried oregano
5ml (1 tsp) dried marjoram
5ml (1 tsp) paprika
15ml (1 tbsp) butter or margarine
60ml (¼ cup) cake flour
325ml (1,5 cups) milk
2,5ml (½ tsp) Aromat seasoning
200g mature Cheddar cheese, grated
500g spinach lasagne

Preheat the oven to 180°C.
Heat the oil in a pan and fry the onions until soft and golden, about 5 minutes.
Add the tomatoes, tomato sauce and purée and cook until you have a thick sauce, about 5 minutes. Add the mince, carrots, peppers, baked beans, oregano, marjoram and paprika and continue to cook over a low heat for 5 minutes.
Melt the butter in a saucepan, add the flour and stir until you have a smooth paste. Gradually add the milk, stirring continuously until a smooth sauce forms. Add the Aromat and half the cheese and stir until incorporated.
In an ovenproof dish alternate layers of the cheese sauce, lasagne and mince mixture, ending with the sauce on top of a layer of lasagne. Top with the remaining cheese and bake until the pasta is cooked and the top is golden brown, about 30 minutes.
Serve hot.

Pot-roast leg of lamb

General Bantu Holomisa says: *I remember when the family used to come down to Qunu and I would get things ready. There was always lamb and it was so tasty. Xoliswa works wonders with everything, but I think that her special skills lie in our traditional cooking and in the preparation of lamb.*

Serves 6 – 8

1,5kg leg of lamb, on the bone
3 garlic cloves, sliced lengthways
750ml (3 cups) water
45ml (3 tbsp) steak and chop spice (mixed spice for barbequed meat)
60ml (¼ cup) lemon juice
5ml (1 tsp) white pepper
15ml (1 tbsp) cake flour

Preheat the oven to 180°C.
Cut thin slits into the lamb with a sharp knife and insert the garlic slivers.
Combine the water, spice, lemon juice and pepper and pour into the bottom of a roasting pan. Place the lamb on top of the liquid and cover with foil.
Roast until the lamb is tender and a brown stock has formed in the pan, about 1 hour. Remove the foil and continue roasting until the lamb is brown, about 15 minutes, adding a little water if it is in danger of burning on the bottom. Remove the meat from the pan and set aside to rest for 15 minutes before carving.
Mix the flour with a little water and add this to the meat juices at the bottom of the roasting pan. Stir over a medium heat on the stove until you have a thick gravy.
Slice the lamb and serve with the gravy and vegetables of your choice.

Roast leg of lamb

Zaziwe Manaway, Nelson Mandela's granddaughter, says: *Every time I go to Grandad's house for lunch or dinner I look forward to Sis' Xoli's food. Every bite you take of her food is like the first time. It's so tasty, flavourful and comforting – she is truly one of the best cooks I know.*

Serves 6 – 8

1,5kg leg of lamb, on the bone
4 garlic cloves, sliced lengthways
60ml (¼ cup) lemon juice
45ml (3 tbsp) steak and chops spice (mixed spice for barbequed meat)
5ml (1 tsp) white pepper
1 whole garlic bulb, cut in half crossways (optional)
1 lemon, quartered (optional)

Preheat the oven to 180°C.
Score thin slits in the meat and insert the garlic slivers.
Mix together the lemon juice, spice and pepper and rub all over the lamb.
Place the lamb in a roasting pan with the halved garlic bulb and lemon wedges, if using, and roast until tender, about 1 hour 30 minutes.
Allow to rest for 15 minutes before carving and serve with vegetables of your choice.

Soy sauce baked lamb chops

Nelson Mandela's close friend, Advocate George Bizos says: *I have known Xoli since the early 1990s. Often when Nelson is alone at lunchtime she phones me and asks if I will have lunch with him. She is a caring person, and knows that companionship for Nelson is very important. My favourite dish from her kitchen is lamb chops with her special sauce.*

Serves 4 – 6

15ml (1 tbsp) olive oil
5ml (1 tsp) crushed garlic
2,5ml (½ teaspoon) steak and chops spice (mixed spice for barbequed meat)
1kg lamb loin chops
250ml (1 cup) tomato sauce (ketchup)
125ml (½ cup) soy sauce
1 medium onion (about 100g), sliced into rings
15ml (1 tbsp) dried oregano

Preheat the oven to 180°C.
Mix together the oil, garlic and meat spice and rub the chops all over with this.
Arrange the chops in an ovenproof dish in a single layer and bake for 20 minutes.
Mix together the tomato sauce, soy sauce, onion and oregano. Pour this mixture over the chops and return to the oven. Bake until the onions have caramelised and a thick, dark sauce has formed, about 15 minutes.
Serve hot with vegetables of your choice.

Mama's meatballs

My mother used to make these for us when I was little. For me they are the taste of home comforts. I liked to help her right from when I was tiny, and I knew that she would serve meatballs with mashed potato, so when I saw her starting to make them I would say, "Can I peel the potatoes?"

Serves 6 – 8

600g lean beef mince
2 medium onions (about 200g), grated
4 medium tomatoes (about 320g), grated
80g cake flour
salt and white pepper, to taste
2 large eggs, lightly beaten
oil, for frying
1 beef stock cube dissolved in 250ml (1 cup) boiling water

Combine the mince with the onions, tomatoes and 60g (½ cup) of the flour. Season and mix well. Mix in the beaten egg and shape the mince mixture into small ovals.

Heat the oil in a pan and fry the meatballs in batches over a medium heat until brown and cooked through, about 5 minutes on each side. Drain on paper towel and set aside to keep warm.

Mix the stock with the remaining flour, stirring until smooth. Pour this liquid into the pan used for the meatballs and stir over a high heat until a rich brown gravy has formed.

Serve the meatballs hot with the gravy poured over.

Cottage pie

Mbuso Mandela, Nelson Mandela's grandson, says: *I remember when I was small I always said I wanted to help make cottage pie, but often I was just hanging around in the kitchen causing chaos. I would say I wanted to learn but when Xoliswa said, 'Put this herb in', or, 'Throw salt in now', I would do the exact opposite and she would end up having to throw out food because I had ruined it. My helping almost always ended with me being chased out of the kitchen.*

Serves 8 – 10

5 medium potatoes (about 1kg), peeled and diced
30ml (2 tbsp) butter
45ml (3 tbsp) sunflower oil
1 medium onion (about 100g), finely chopped
30ml (2 tbsp) fresh parsley, finely chopped
10ml (2 tsp) dried oregano
5ml (1 tsp) dried marjoram
30ml (2 tbsp) tomato paste
2kg beef mince
salt and white pepper, to taste

Cook the potatoes in boiling salted water until soft, about 15 minutes. Drain and mash with the butter.

Preheat the oven to 180˚C.

Heat the oil in a pan and fry the onion until soft and golden, about 5 minutes.

Add the parsley, oregano, marjoram and tomato paste. Mix well and cook over a low heat until thickened, about 5 minutes.

Add the mince, season and cook until browned, about 5 minutes.

Transfer the mince mixture to an oven dish and top with the mashed potato. Bake in the oven until golden brown, about 20 minutes. Serve hot.

Pork chops with mushroom sauce

Gloria Nocanda, Xoliswa's friend and fellow chef, says: *Sis' Xoli, she's such a sweet person. When Tata told me he wanted an extra somebody to help me in the kitchen I thought of her immediately. You see, we're home girls. Both from Queenstown and so we can both cook Tata's traditional food. And she's got such a nice gentle quality – the kids responded well to her from the beginning. I don't know how she does it, but she can work miracles – anyone can get a kid to eat cupcakes, but she could get those kids to eat anything!*

Serves 8

8 x 100g pork chops
5ml (1 tsp) mixed spice for chicken
10ml (2 tsp) dried thyme
salt and white pepper, to taste
30ml (2 tbsp) olive oil
2 medium onions, sliced into thick rounds
2 garlic cloves, finely chopped
250g white button mushrooms, thickly sliced
500ml (2 cups) fresh cream
30ml (2 tbsp) cake flour
60ml (¼ cup) water

Preheat the oven to 180C.
Rub the chops all over with the chicken spice, thyme, salt and pepper.
Heat the oil in a large pan and fry the chops until golden brown on both sides.
Transfer the chops to an oven dish and bake for 20 minutes.
While the chops are cooking, fry the onion in the pan used for the chops until soft and golden, about 5 minutes. Add the garlic and mushrooms and cook for 2 minutes.
Add the cream and cook over a medium heat until reduced by one third.
Mix the flour and water to make a smooth paste and add to the mushroom mixture. Cook over a low heat, stirring continuously until smooth, about 5 minutes. Season.
Add the chops to the sauce, cover and cook in the oven for 15 minutes.
Serve hot.

Spiced beef stew

Nelson Mandela's friend and former bodyguard, Vusi Zulu, says: *I remember when we were first in the Presidency, right after the inauguration. Those security guards that had been brought in from the old order, they needed liberation. They were so unused to being treated well. On the first day Sis' Xoli offered them stew for lunch and they were amazed. Until then they had had to buy their own food. She liberated the staff by showing them that we were going to treat all with respect.*

Serves 8 – 10

1kg beef chuck, cleaned and cut into 6cm cubes
2 beef stock cubes
2 medium onions (about 200g), finely chopped
8 baby (new) potatoes, peeled and halved
4 large carrots (about 300g), peeled and sliced
250g green beans, sliced
2 medium tomatoes (about 150g), peeled and grated
5ml (1 tsp) fresh thyme, leaves only
3 garlic cloves, finely chopped
4 bay leaves
2,5ml (½ tsp) cayenne pepper
salt and white pepper, to taste

Put the beef into a deep pot and cover with water. Bring to the boil, then reduce the heat and cook over a low heat until tender, about 1 hour. Add the remaining ingredients and cook until the vegetables are soft, about 30 minutes.
Serve hot.

Bread and dessert

The blessing of breaking bread

Umbhako (pot bread)

Sarah Mabulela, Mandela family housekeeper, says: *I don't know what she does, but this woman has a secret way with pots. She's a magician.*

Makes 1 large pot-shaped loaf

butter or margarine, for greasing the pot
780g (6 cups) cake flour
7,5ml (1,5 tsp) salt
5ml (1 tsp) sugar
10g (1 sachet) instant dry yeast
lukewarm water, as needed

You will need a 2-litre, cast-iron pot with a tight-fitting lid. Generously grease both the lid and the pot with the butter or margarine.

Sieve the flour and salt into a bowl and mix in the sugar and yeast. Gradually mix in enough lukewarm water to form a stiff dough (the amount will vary according to the humidity in the air). Knead until firm but elastic.

Place the dough in a lightly oiled bowl, cover with a wet cloth and set aside in a warm place until doubled in size, about 1 hour.

Knock down the dough and knead again, then roll it into a ball and place in the pot. Cover the pot with the lid and set aside until the dough has once more doubled in size.

Once the dough has risen almost to the top of the pot, put the pot on the stove over a low heat and cook with the lid on until the bread has set, about 30 minutes.

Take the bread out of the pot, turn it over, return to the pot, cover and cook for a further 30 minutes so that the bread has a golden-brown crust on the top and the bottom. (Traditionally this bread is made over a fire. If you make it over a fire, place some coals on top of the pot lid so that the bread cooks evenly on all sides.)

Serve with butter and apricot jam.

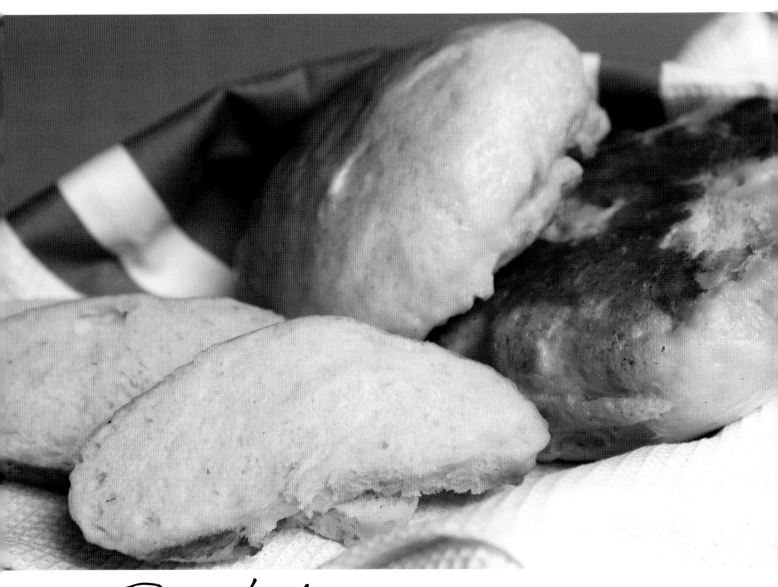

Dombolo (dumplings)

Ndaba Mandela, Nelson Mandela's grandson, says: *I love Xoliswa's dombolo dumplings. When the sauce of the stew goes into the dough, that's the best. For me that's the classic taste of my grandfather's house, when I taste that I know I am being taken care of.*

Serves 8 – 10

650g (5 cups) cake flour
5ml (1 tsp) salt
5ml (1 tsp) sugar
10g (1 sachet) instant dry yeast
625ml (2 ½ cups) lukewarm water
30ml (2 tbsp) butter

Cook's Note: Dough will require more – or less – water depending on the weather, so adjust according to your heat and humidity conditions.

When covering with a lid, leave a small gap for some of the steam to escape.

Sieve the flour and salt into a bowl and mix in the sugar and yeast. Gradually add the water, mixing until a soft dough is formed.
Knead the dough until smooth and elastic, then cover the bowl with plastic wrap and set aside in a warm place until doubled in size, about 1 hour.
Melt the butter in a pot. Roll the dough into balls the size of your palm.
Place the balls of dough in the melted butter and pour boiling water into the pot to a depth of 2cm. Cover with a lid and cook over medium heat until the dumplings are cooked through, about 20 minutes. As the water evaporates the butter will begin to fry the base of the dumplings – keep an eye on them to check that they don't burn and add a little more water if necessary.
Serve hot with a meat dish such as umleqwa.

Potato bread

I served this dish when we went to Shambala resort with Mark Shuttleworth. Mark ate well and you could see Madiba was pleased he was enjoying his food. As he was eating his last mouthful, Madiba said jokingly to him, "You know, Mark, I am not rich like you. You must understand that even if you like the cooking from my kitchen, you mustn't steal my people. I can't pay them like you can, but I need them."

Serves 6 – 8

4 medium potatoes (about 800g), peeled and grated
2 medium onions (about 200g), grated
2 large eggs, beaten
40g (⅓ cup) cake flour
5ml (1 tsp) Aromat seasoning
10ml (2 tsp) baking powder,
125ml (½ cup) cooking oil
salt and white pepper, to taste

Preheat the oven to 180°C.
Mix the potatoes and onions well together and mix in the eggs. Add the flour, Aromat and baking powder and mix well.
Heat the oil in an oven tray.
Pour the potato mixture into the hot oil in the tray and bake in the oven until cooked through and brown, about 40 minutes. It will rise like bread and have a muffin-like texture.
Allow to cool a little before slicing into squares. Season and serve.

Strawberry trifle

When he turned 80, Madiba started to like ice cream and custard. Before he used to say to the children, "I don't eat much dessert, mainly fruit." But now when I serve it to the kids he will say, "Can I taste that?" as if he just wants to check it, but you find that a "taste" means eating the whole thing!

Serves 6 – 8

80g (1 packet) strawberry jelly
100g (1 packet) vanilla instant pudding
250ml (1 cup) sour cream
250ml (1 cup) milk
5ml (1 tsp) orange zest
1 vanilla Swiss roll, sliced
500ml (2 cups) double cream, whipped
500g strawberries, leaves removed

Make the jelly according to the packet instructions and set aside in the fridge.
Combine the instant pudding, sour cream, milk and orange zest. Beat until the mixture thickens. Set aside in the fridge.
Once the jelly and pudding are both almost set, start to assemble the trifle:
In a large bowl or individual bowls, alternate layers of Swiss roll, pudding mixture and jelly, ending with a layer of the pudding mixture.
Cover and refrigerate for at least 2 hours.
Top with the whipped cream, arrange the strawberries on top and serve.

Rice pudding

Dr Ike Kwame Amuah, Nelson Mandela's's son-in-law, says: *I always eat more than what the stomach can take. No regret though, if I come across as a glutton in the Mandela household ... what a wicked delight.*

Serves 4 – 6

375 ml (1,5 cups) cooked rice, cooled
80g (½ cup) raisins
80g (½ cup) sultanas
250ml (1 cup) fresh cream or evaporated milk
5ml (1 tsp) ground cinnamon

Preheat the oven to 180°C.
Mix all the ingredients together.
Bake in the oven until golden brown, about 20 minutes.
Serve hot.

Citrus pudding

Basetsana Kumalo, businesswoman and Mandela family friend, says: *Any opportunity to break bread with Tata is cause for celebration. Just to be in his presence makes you count your blessings. You could have tea and bread and it would still stand out as the most special meal.*

Serves 6 – 8

60ml (¼ cup) butter, melted
200g tennis biscuits, crushed
400ml frozen orange juice concentrate
5ml (1 tsp) lemon juice
250ml (1 cup) fresh cream, beaten until soft peaks form
4 large egg whites, beaten until stiff
5ml (1 tsp) lemon zest

In a glass dish, mix together the butter and the biscuits for the crust. Press into the base and sides of the dish.

Place the orange juice concentrate and lemon juice in a bowl or jug. Fold in the cream and egg whites and pour this mixture over the biscuit base.

Sprinkle the lemon zest on top and refrigerate until set, about 1 hour.

Serve garnished with finely grated lemon rind (optional).

Drinks

Aunt Nobandla's ginger beer

Aunt Nobandla's ginger beer

My aunt Nobandla's ginger beer is famous in Queenstown. When I was about 10 years old I used to help her make and sell this brew. It was my job to pour the fizzing ginger into the bottles. She sold it for 12 cents a bottle, but if I poured nicely I was allowed to have the occasional bottle for myself.

Makes approximately 20 litres

20 litres lukewarm water
50g ground ginger
2,5kg brown sugar
2 x 10g packets tartaric acid (cream of tartar)
1 x 10g (1 sachet) packet instant dry yeast

Mix all the ingredients together in a deep bucket and leave to stand overnight. Foam will form on top so be sure that your bucket is deep enough to contain this increase in volume.
Strain the foaming ginger beer and pour into bottles.
Serve cold.

Amasi (sour milk)

General Bantu Holomisa says: *Xoliswa really is a remarkable cook. She makes our traditional recipes with such love and skill. If only there were more such cooks in our land.*

Serves 4

1 litre milk, fresh from the cow (i.e. unpasteurised and never refrigerated)
1 hollowed-out calabash, with a corn-cob stopper

Put the milk in the calabash and seal with the stopper, but check that the stopper is not too tight as the fermentation process will release gas, which can cause the calabash to burst if pressure builds up.

Leave the calabash at room temperature until the milk has separated into curds (*ingqaka*) and whey (*inthoya*). In summer this will take 3 to 4 days; in winter it can take up to 10 days.

Remove the stopper and pour out the whey. Scoop out the remaining curds. Some people then remix the whey and curds but Madiba likes to discard the whey and just eat the curds.

Cook's Note:
Also known as an *iselwa*, a calabash is made from a hollowed out, dried gourd. It infuses organic flavour into the *amasi*. You can make it in a glass or clay container but it will not taste the same.

Amarhewu (fermented maize drink)

When I make amarhewu I feel the influence of the many generations of Xhosa women who have stirred the pots that came before us. Recipes like these are a gift from the past to the present and the future. They link where we are with where we came from.

Serves 6 – 8

1kg maize meal
2,5 litres lukewarm water
sugar, optional, to taste

Soak the maize meal in the water overnight, which will start the fermentation process.
Place the maize and water in a pot over low heat and cook until a soft porridge has formed, about 30 minutes.
Pour the porridge into a bowl and allow to cool. The porridge will be slightly sour due to the fermentation process.
Although the texture of amarhewu is a personal matter, it must be pourable, so add at least 2 cups of additional water and beat vigorously to remove any lumps.
Pour and serve. Traditionally amarhewu should be sour, but you can add sugar if you prefer it sweet.

Conversion tables

Weights/measures	
Metric	Imperial
30g	1 ounce
250g	8 ounces
550g	1lb
1kg	2,2lb
600ml	1 pint
1,25 litres	2 pints (1 quart)

Temperatures		
C	F	Gas
140	275	2
160	325	3
180	350	3
200	400	4

Statement of love, affection and gratitude from Nkosi Zwelivelile Mandela

There are no words to describe the enormity of the contribution that Sis' Xoli has made to the Mandela family, but I am going to try to express my appreciation to this dear and good lady. For me she symbolises the strong role of women in this family. She has warmth in her heart, but also power. Everyone in my family has their own favourite recipe, and there is no doubt that she has brought a selection of fine tastes to us, but I think it is important to point out that her role is so much more than simply the sum of what she puts on the dinner table.

First, I want to thank her for the way that she made my grandfather's house a home. She has always brought to us a mother's love. With her, in every meal she has made for us, we have known we were cared for. Second, I want her to know that my brothers and I are aware that making our lives better and easier was not always so simple for her. When I first came to know her I was a teenager and my brothers were mere children. We were so young that we didn't realise that she wasn't just ours. For a long time we didn't really understand that she had her own family but now that we are adults we recognise that we owe Sis' Xoli's children such a debt of gratitude. They shared their mother with us and we are men today because of her guidance.

I know I speak for my whole family when I say thank you, Sis' Xoli, for everything. Thank you for the trifle and the sweet chicken and all the other delicious foods, but most of all thank you for the care and generosity with which you shaped us and helped us to become the people that we are today.

Nkosi Zwelivelile Mandela

OPRAH WINFREY

Jan 8'02

Xoliswa —

Thank you for making my stay at Qunu a happy, delicious and comfortable time. I will never forget.

Opal Winfrey

Oprah Winfrey with Graça Machel and Nelson Mandela at his 90th birthday celebrations in London, 2007.

Photograph: 46664 / Richard Young

Nelson Mandela Centre of Memory Publications Programme

Books about or related to Nelson Mandela constitute a substantial industry. The Nelson Mandela Centre of Memory's publications programme, inaugurated in 2005 with the publication of *A Prisoner in the Garden: Opening Nelson Mandela's Prison Archive*, seeks to support or deliver quality publications in areas not heavily represented already by that industry. Three areas are prioritised: deep archival research aimed at delivering archival materials in marketable form – within a frame of 'taking archives to the people'; narratives and materials designed specifically to reach young people; and projects aimed at foregrounding the 'hidden voices' in Mr Mandela's life. The programme is supported by the Centre's in-house research capacity, informed by extraordinary access to archival materials, and shaped by public education rather than commercial imperatives.

Ruth Rensburg
Nelson Mandela Centre of Memory

NELSON MANDELA CENTRE OF MEMORY
at the Nelson Mandela Foundation
Living the legacy

Nelson Mandela reads a booklet on the role of women in the struggle produced by the Nelson Mandela Centre of Memory. Looking on is one of his assistants, Vimla Naidoo.

Photograph: Nelson Mandela Foundation / Matthew Willman

Glossary

Amafutha enkuku	chicken fat left over from cooking (like schmaltz)
Amarhewu	a drink made from fermented maize
Amasi	sour milk
Andilohashe	I'm not a horse
Aromat	a South African brand of seasoning, mostly consisting of MSG: as an alternative, use salt and pepper according to your taste
Bobotie	a dish of Cape Malay origin, made with mince, egg custard, raisins and chutney
Boerewors	farmer's sausage
Inconco	porridge made from fermented maize and water
Iselwa	a calabash, made from a gourd, for brewing amasi
Isidudu	thin, runny maize meal porridge
Isophu	soup, specifically one made with sugar beans and white maize
Madiba	is Nelson Mandela's clan name and is the name by which he best likes to be called
Magwinya	fritters or fatcakes
Maize meal	finely ground maize (corn); different brands have different weights, which may affect the consistency; best use the most finely ground you can find
Nkosi	Chief, lord
Pap	maize meal cooked until it is stiff
Samp	crushed maize
Tata	means "father" and is used for respected elders such as Nelson Mandela and Walter Sisulu
Tshakalaka	a spicy relish made of vegetables, sometimes spelt "chakalaka" on commercially available tins
Ukutya kwasekhaya	home food
Ulusu	tripe
Umbhako	pot bread
Umfino	maize meal porridge with spinach
Umhluzi	a traditional meat gravy
Umkhuphu	beans with maize meal
Umleqwa	a farm chicken
Umngqusho	samp and beans
Umphokoqo	crumbly maize meal porridge and sour milk
Umqa wekhaphetshu	stiff maize meal porridge with curried cabbage
Umsila wenkomo	oxtail stew
Umxhaxha	a dish of corn and pumpkin

Index

Gem squash
    Filled gem squash   66

Lamb
    Pot-roast leg of lamb   126
    Roast leg of lamb   128
    Soy-sauce baked lamb chops   130
    Ulusu (tripe)   120

Lentils
    Brown and green lentil soup   34

Maize (corn)
    Amarhewu (fermented maize drink)   160
    Isophu (sugar bean and white
      maize soup)   28
    Umfino (maize meal porridge
      with spinach)   50
    Umkhuphu (beans with maize meal)   56
    Umngqusho (samp and beans)   48
    Umphokoqo (crumbly maize meal
      porridge and sour milk)   52
    Umqa wekhaphetshu (stiff maize
      meal porridge with curried
      cabbage)   46
    Umxhaxha (corn and pumpkin)   54

Mangoes
    Curried mango rice salad   76

Mushrooms
    Chicken and mushroom casserole   112
    Pork chops with mushroom sauce   136

Pasta
    Lasagne   124
    Seafood spaghetti stir-fry   92

Peanut butter
    Peanut butter and spinach soup   40

Pineapple
    Carrot and pineapple salad   80

Pork
    Pork chops with mushroom sauce   136

Porridge
    Umfino (maize meal porridge
      with spinach)   50
    Umphokoqo (crumbly maize meal
      porridge and sour milk)   52
    Umqa wekhaphetshu (stiff maize
      meal porridge with curried
      cabbage)   46

Potatoes
    Creamy potatoes   82
    Potato bread   146
    Potato latkes   62

Prawns/seafood
    Late-start starter   88
    Paella   94
    Prawn curry   90
    Prawn soup   42

Pumpkin
    Pumpkin fritters   64
    Umxhaxha (corn and pumpkin)   54

Relish
    Tshakalaka (spicy relish)   58

Rice
    Curried mango rice salad   76
    Paella   94
    Rice pudding   150
    Savoury rice   78

Salads
    Aubergine salad   68
    Carrot and pineapple salad   80
    Curried mango rice salad   76

Samp
    Umngqusho (samp and beans)   48

Soups
    Brown and green lentil soup   34
    Butternut soup   30
    Chicken soup   38
    Isophu (sugar bean and white
      maize soup)   28

Pea soup   26
Peanut butter and spinach soup   40
Prawn soup   42
Spinach soup   36
Vegetable soup   32

Spinach
Creamed spinach   74
Peanut butter and spinach soup   40
Spinach soup   36
Umfino (maize meal porridge
    with spinach)   50

Strawberries
Strawberry trifle   150

Tripe
Ulusu (tripe)   120

Turkey
Orange turkey   116

Vegetable dishes
Aubergine salad   68
Creamed spinach   74
Creamy potatoes   82
Filled gem squash   66
Fried butternut   70
Lemon Brussels sprouts   72
Potato latkes   62
Pumpkin fritters   64
Savoury rice   78
Tshakalaka (spicy relish)   58
Umfino (maize meal porridge
    with spinach)   50
Umkhuphu (beans with maize meal)   56
Umngqusho (samp and beans)   48
Umphokoqo (crumbly maize meal
    porridge and sour milk)   52
Umqa wekhaphetshu (stiff maize
    meal porridge with curried
    cabbage)   46
Umxhaxha (corn and pumpkin)   54